JOURNEY TO THE ROCK

FOUNDATIONS OF FAITH - DEVOTIONAL JOURNAL

ALL NATIONS INTERNATIONAL   TERESA SKINNER

GORDON SKINNER   AGNES I NUMER

ASHLEY FLORES   ONOH KESANDU NWANKWO

WITH
FAITH CHIDINMA METCHIE

Journey to the Rock
Foundations of Faith - Devotional Journal
Isaiah 58 Mobile Training Institute

ISBN: 978-1-955759-10-6

Cover Art: Julian Peter V. Arias and Eve Lorraine Rivers Trinidad

Isaiah 58 Mobile Training Institute
is available for use in training programs.
For more information or to
order additional copies of this manual:

email: is58mti@gmail.com
contact us: www.all-nations.org
online course: is58mti.org

We dedicate this manual:
To those who wanted to know... but never had a teacher.
To those who looked for the vision... so that they could run with it.
To those who want to know "What's Next?"
To those who knew they were teachers... but did not know what to teach.
To those who are looking for Christ in Us the Hope of Glory!
May this manual reveal to you Jesus Christ and
May the peace that He has ordained for you be with you always.

Look for the arrow: quizzes, puzzles and special information.
Answers on in back of the book.

CONTENTS

WHO IS GOD?

We think God is created like us... **He is not... God is a Spirit.**

God is a triune being. Meaning that there are 3 in 1. God the Father God the Son and God the Holy Spirit.

We are **created like Him.**

God was... Even **before** we were created. He has no beginning and no end. **God made** everything; heaven and earth and all living things. God also made man.

GOD IS THE CREATOR

In the beginning, God created the Heavens and the earth in only seven days:

Day 1: God created Light and separated the Light from the Darkness.
Day 2: God created the heavens.
Day 3: God created Earth, sea, and vegetation.
Day 4: God created Sun, Moon, and Stars.
Day 5: God created Birds and Sea Animals.

Day 6: God created Land Animals and Humans.
Day 7: God rested.

When God created man, he made him out of the dust of the earth. After God formed man, He breathed into him and man became a living, breathing creature. This makes us special to God.

> *"The Lord is full of grace and pity; not quickly angry, but great in mercy."*

PSALM 145:8 BBE

WHICH DAY DID GOD CREATE...

Answers are in the back of the book

- Sun Moon and Stars
- The Heavens
- Rest
- Earth, Sea, Vegetation
- Light
- Land Animals and Adam
- Birds and Sea Animals

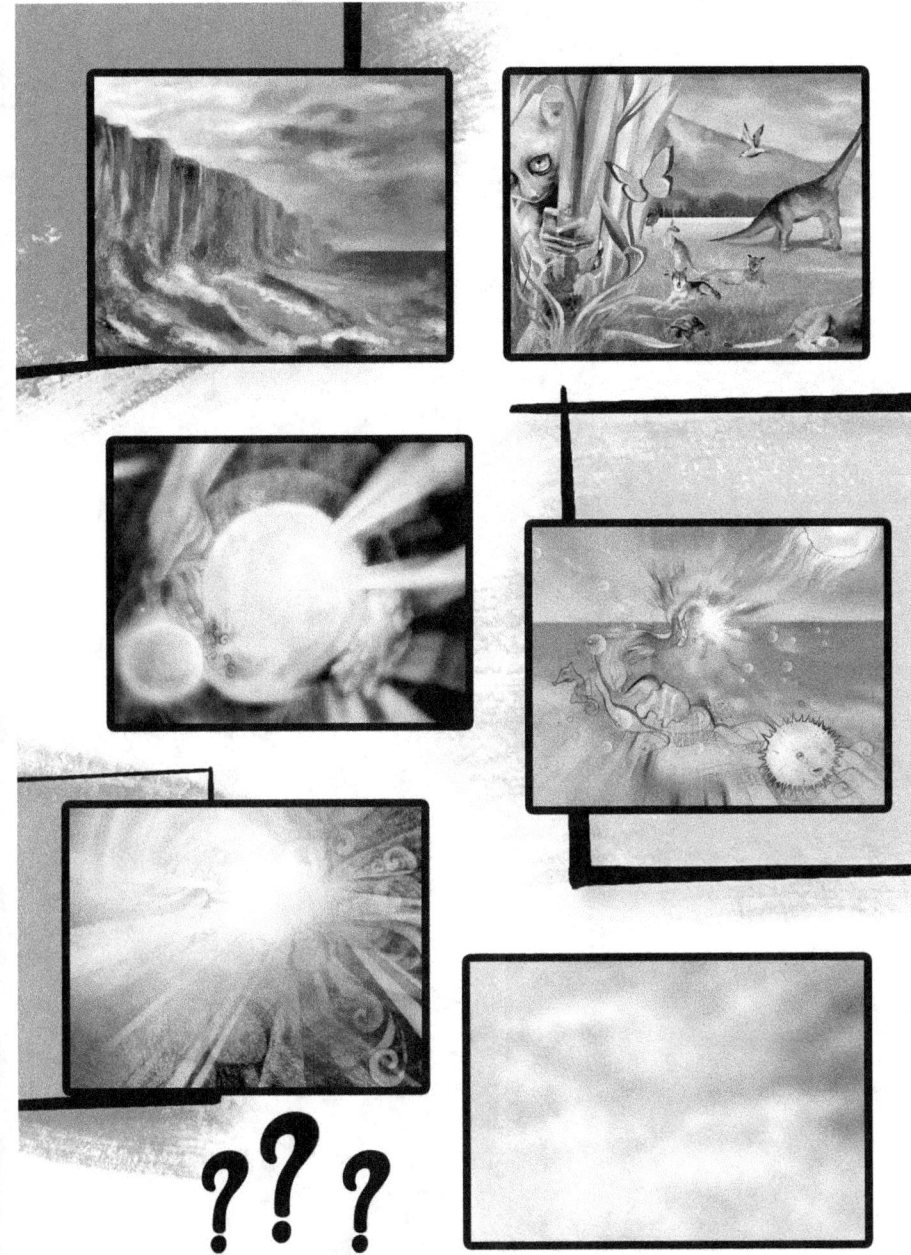

God wants the best for you. The Bible is God's word written for man to understand His ways and His commands.

God is merciful, gracious, slow to anger, abundant in loving kindness and truth.

After God created the world, He made a garden and put a man in it.

Imagine this place: the most beautiful garden, or park where there is no pain, suffering, or torment! Everything you need to eat grows naturally there for you. The animals get along peacefully. No one fights or is angry; there are no bad attitudes and no unkind words. God and His people walked and talked in the garden when the evenings became cool. Everything was perfect.

This is what God made in the beginning, for the people He loved.

WATCH THE VIDEO:

Genesis Creation

https://youtu.be/8YffLe9yeWg

Learn more about Biblical Creation? [1]

---

1. Read: ***A Study of God's Creation:*** *Filled with Purpose, Direction, and Consequence by Roland Beard or visit CreationStudyHelps on YouTube.*

FILL IN THE WORDS BELOW

The first one is done for you.

A	T	D	N	I	G	H	T	G	I	Y	G	H	L
T	L	N	G	N	I	S	I	D	A	K	I	N	S
L	I	M	N	A	I	G	O	D	R	S	T	A	T
A	V	G	N	L	R	L	N	R	O	P	S	H	S
S	I	F	I	I	B	D	H	N	M	S	G	O	T
L	N	H	S	G	R	P	E	A	N	R	A	N	V
S	G	G	T	H	E	E	S	N	A	F	S	N	B
F	T	R	A	T	A	A	S	S	S	I	N	I
H	H	H	R	I	T	R	G	A	L	F	I	S	E
M	I	D	S	I	H	T	S	N	A	A	G	S	H
O	N	N	U	G	N	H	N	R	M	B	E	R	L
O	G	S	N	S	M	P	A	L	I	H	N	H	H
N	S	K	D	A	U	P	L	A	N	T	S	O	I
T	N	Y	S	I	N	N	S	N	A	S	I	N	P

Day	Garden	Living Things
Breath	Animals	Stars
Sun	Plants	God
Fish	Light	Night
Sky	Moon	Earth

DEVO DAY 1:

WHO IS GOD?

God made everything that is living, and He made every human on the planet. Not only did He create everything in 6 days, but each thing He made, He called good. That means when He created you, He saw His work in making you good!

Maybe you're thinking "Well, 'good' isn't the word I would use to describe myself, or other people!" What it means is that God was happy with His work in creating the earth, animals, water, sky and the humans that live on the Earth. That means when He formed you, He looked at you and saw that His work was complete, with no mistakes.

After reading this chapter, how has it changed the way you see God? How do you see yourself and others?

Notes

Where Does God Live?

Where does God Live?

WHERE DOES GOD LIVE?

God is a Spirit He does not have a body like ours.

He lives in heaven and we can invite Him to live in our hearts.

God has His own kingdom.

God has His own culture and His own way of expressing Himself.

We cannot control Him. He is God.

WHERE DO YOU THINK GOD LIVES?

Write your answer here:

_____

_____

_____

_____

_____

_____

LET'S CONTINUE THE JOURNEY:

Safari

Vwayaj

Journey

Irin ajo

Viaje

njem

Tafiya

paglalakbay

Dos Iponawon

WATCH THE VIDEO:

What Color is God

https://youtu.be/Yr0K73ZA9JM

WHAT COLOR IS GOD?

God is Light, Light is all colors.
God is not white, brown, yellow, or black.
God is all colors. We are ALL made like Him.

It is important that we know who God is and that He wants to walk and talk with us. God wants His people to know Him.

MEMORY VERSE:

He made known his ways unto Moses, his acts unto the children of Israel.

PSALM 103:7

DEVO DAY 2:
WHAT COLOR IS GOD?

Each of us look different from one another. No two people look like exactly alike, not even twins! The way we look, talk and think shows us a different aspect of who God is, and He loves variety! Knowing this important because it helps us treat everyone around us with respect and love — **because God made them too!**

Find the words in the puzzle below. Look up the countries you don't know, to learn about them!

N	K	S	E	N	I	P	P	I	L	I	H	P	R
I	R	U	S	S	I	A	D	A	N	A	C	A	I
N	A	T	I	V	E	A	M	E	R	I	C	A	N
A	M	C	L	B	B	R	A	Z	I	L	E	H	S
P	N	H	E	E	A	D	N	A	L	I	A	H	T
G	E	I	A	L	U	R	E	P	Y	N	N	G	M
A	D	L	R	E	P	I	B	A	B	D	E	E	E
E	R	E	S	E	O	E	D	A	I	I	D	R	X
E	T	H	I	O	P	I	A	Y	D	A	E	M	I
C	N	K	E	N	Y	A	I	D	J	O	W	A	C
N	N	A	M	I	B	I	A	S	N	A	S	N	O
A	Z	A	E	J	O	R	D	A	N	A	P	Y	R
R	A	A	R	G	E	N	T	I	N	A	G	A	U
F	S	E	T	A	T	S	D	E	T	I	N	U	N

- Mexico - Uganda - Peru - England
- Israel - Russia - Japan - Thailand
- Nigeria - Liberia - Sweden - Brazil
- Canada - Jordan - Australia - India
- Philippines - Kenya - Chile
- Native American - Ethiopia

CREATED IN GOD'S IMAGE?

WHAT DOES IT MEAN TO BE CREATED IN GOD'S IMAGE?

When someone says, "You are like your Father," they are saying that you talk, walk, think and act like your Father, or that you have special abilities like he does. When God created us, He gave us special abilities and qualities like He has.

We have spiritual abilities to know God, to talk with Him, and to be aware of His presence.

We have free will – we can choose.

We have creativity – we can create.

We have intelligence – we can think, learn, and understand.

We have authority – we can rule (control, organize).

DEVO DAY 3:

CREATED IN GOD'S IMAGE

It seems a hard thing to understand: this amazing God that created the universe and all living things in it, the stars and planets in space, also created each of us! Not only did He create us, but each of us in our uniqueness represents a different part of who God is. Our creativity, our intelligence, our laughs, how we love and treat other people, our characteristics, our gifts and talents, even how we look, shows the world a piece of God. In a world so divided, we have forgotten that each of us were created by God, in God's image, for His purposes.

JOURNAL PROMPT:

How can you use your gifts, talents and life to show the world who He is?

Journal

WHO IS GOD'S ONE ENEMY?

God has one enemy; he is evil and he hates God and hates His people. This enemy will do everything in his wicked power to stop God's plan. This enemy's name is Satan or the Devil.

He came to the Garden of Eden as a serpent, to lie to Adam and Eve. Adam and Eve listened to Satan and sinned. Then they could no longer walk and talk with God. The world became an ugly place to live because of sin.

God told them if they disobeyed, this would happen.. This is called "Death."

NOW, men are born with the tendency to sin... It is in their DNA.

People lost the strength to create or choose what is right, and they became slaves to sin. They are separated from God.

God wants you to become one of His children. God loves you and wants you to know Him and learn His ways. He will save you from the devil's lies and the bondage of sin.

God wants to restore to you His special characteristics that He gave to Adam.

God wants to bring you back into "the image of God." You will again be one of His people and **He will be your God.**

You will learn to know Him, walk with Him, and talk with Him.

DEVO DAY 4:

WHO IS GOD'S ONE ENEMY?

There's a hard truth that we all have to face sometime: there is God and there is the devil. If you aren't serving God, how are you serving? The Bible calls the devil the father of lies, and having no truth at all!

...He was a murderer from the beginning, not

holding to the truth, for there is no truth in him.
When he lies, he speaks his native language, for
he is a liar and the father of lies.

JOHN 8:44 NIV

God wants each of us to become one His children and have the same sweet relationship God had with Adam and Eve before they sinned. One way to become His child, is to know who His enemy is and stay away from him!

JOURNAL PROMPT:

Make a list of things that separate you from Him.

What can you do to stay way from those things?

Make a list of things that help you draw near to God.

How can you make these things habits in your life?

Journal

Think outside the box

WHAT IS SIN?

Ask yourself these questions:

- Is it something that God says is wrong?
- Does it make you sick or unhealthy?
- Do you always have to tell yourself it is right?
- Did you feel guilty/bad when you started doing it?
- Do you have to keep yourself from doing it?
- Is it sin?

SIN SEPARATES US FROM GOD.

God wants to bring us back to Him, so He can walk and talk with us like He did in the Garden of Eden with Adam and Eve.

Let's be honest: it's not always comfortable to admit we've been wrong. We try to find ways to excuse what we do, instead of admitting it's wrong. Maybe you've heard someone say "It's only a *little* lie. It's not that big of a deal!" Maybe you've even said it yourself! But...have you ever thought about how God sees sin? He doesn't care if its big or small. If its sin, its sin!

SIN is also NOT DOING what we were created to do.

God gives us commands and instructions to follow for our own good. It is to make us into the person He created us to be. It is also to benefit others.

WHEN WE DO NOT OBEY GOD, IT IS SIN.

~

JOURNAL PROMPT:

Has God asked you to do something?

_____

_____

_____

_____

_____

_____

_____

PUZZLE: IS IT SIN?

FIND THE WORDS:

Meekness

Fornication

Angry Outbursts

Murders

Wild Parties

False Teachings

Hatred

Fighting

Love

Abuse Of Drugs

Witchcraft

Drunkenness

Selfishness

Goodness

Idolatry

Lust

Lying

Envy
Faith
Joy

G	S	T	F	A	R	C	H	C	T	I	W	S	D
F	A	L	S	E	T	E	A	C	H	I	N	G	S
I	G	N	I	Y	L	M	U	R	D	E	R	S	S
Y	J	I	D	O	L	A	T	R	Y	A	R	S	S
G	O	O	D	N	E	S	S	F	A	I	T	H	E
E	N	V	Y	F	C	L	O	V	E	N	I	H	L
I	S	G	U	R	D	F	O	E	S	U	B	A	F
E	L	N	O	I	T	A	C	I	N	R	O	F	I
S	Y	S	H	A	T	R	E	D	A	E	N	L	S
W	I	L	D	P	A	R	T	I	E	S	E	W	H
N	H	G	N	I	T	H	G	I	F	N	R	S	N
M	E	E	K	N	E	S	S	T	T	S	U	L	E
A	N	G	R	Y	O	U	T	B	U	R	S	T	S
E	K	E	D	R	U	N	K	E	N	N	E	S	S

Answers are in the back of the book.

WHAT DO WE DO IF WE SIN?

We must look at our sin the way God sees it.

WHAT ARE WE SUPPOSED TO DO ABOUT SIN?

- Run from sin!
- Say yes to God.
- Say no to the devil.
- Get close to God.
- Keep your heart clean.
- Make up your mind: No more!
- Ask God to forgive you from your sin.
- Let God into your life.

DEVO DAY 5:

WHAT IS SIN?

Sin is what drove Adam and Eve out of the garden of Eden. Before that, Adam and Eve walked and talked to God face to face in the garden. They had a close relationship.

Sin isn't just doing the wrong things, but also not doing the things God created you to do. So...what do we do about sin?

Prayer: Lord, I no longer want to do things that keep me from You. Thank for you for showing me ways to walk away from the things that destroy my relationship with You! I choose to love and serve You. Amen.

JOURNAL PROMPT:

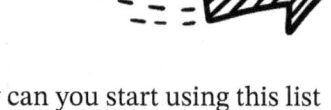

Look at the list under "What are we supposed to do about sin?" How can you start using this list to turn from sin in your own life?

WHO IS JESUS?

We have all sinned, so now what can we do? Sin separates from the God who made us.

Sometimes we feel separated and must go on a journey to find God.

WHY are we separated from God?

God, the Creator of the Universe, walked with Adam and Eve in the garden.

Adam sinned. Adam's sin separated him and all of his descendants from God.

Adam and Eve became cursed and alone.

WHO IS JESUS?

JESUS brings us back to God. God sent His only Son, Jesus, to die on the cross for us, is because we are weak to sin.

Jesus is the Son of God.

Jesus is Emmanuel 'God on Earth.'

God sent Jesus to become **"The Ultimate Sacrifice." Jesus became** man to Save man.

Jesus became the sacrifice for our sins. Jesus died for our sins, so we didn't have to die without God.

Jesus not only washes away our sin, but takes from us all past, present, and future sins and works in our hearts that we may not continue to live in sin. When we ask God to forgive us, God gives us power over sin.

JESUS' ULTIMATE SACRIFICE MAKES HIM OUR SAVIOR.

DEVO DAY 6:

WHO IS JESUS?

We have lots of things that can live in our hearts: dreams, hopes, fears, joy, pain. Some things we don't mind living in our hearts, good memories, our hopes, joy. But there are other things that live in our hearts that we wish we could forget: shame, anger, fear, sadness.

There is One who can live in hearts that changes how we think, talk and act. He helps us manage our emotions, love those around us, and heals the broken, painful parts in our hearts and minds. But He only can live and stay in your heart if you ask Him.

Have you asked Him yet?

JOURNAL PROMPT:

Write a prayer, asking Jesus to come and live in your heart.

Tell Him the things you would like Him to help you with, and how you can help Jesus build His kingdom.

WHAT IS REPENTANCE?

We now realize we have a problem. Sin has separated us from God.

How do we get to where God is taking us?

WHAT is the problem?

Because of Adam and Eve's sin, everyone born is separated from God!

WHAT is the Solution?

Repentance!

HUMAN REGRET is not repentance

We cannot just feel guilty when we do something wrong. We must ask for change so we don't continue to sin. We must have godly sorrow.

Feeling guilty is not repentance

Repentance is looking at the sin we have done... God's way. When we do, we become sorry for what we have done, and we don't do it again. **Sometimes, we have to run from sin.**

GODLY SORROW – Godly sorrow leads to doing something about the situation.

Do you have something that you would like to repent from?

Have you asked Jesus the Ultimate Sacrifice to come into your heart and give you a new life? Have you found yourself ignoring sin and instead doing what you think is right and not looking to what God says is right? Maybe you would like to pray and ask Him for forgiveness. Begin that new life right now.

REPENTANCE; A RIGHT HEART

Isaiah 57:15; Hebrews 3:12-15

MEMORY VERSE:

> *"My brothers, take care that there is not by chance in any one of you an evil heart without belief, turning away from the living God:"*

HEBREWS 3:12 BBE

Repentance is a sincere change in one's thinking and attitude, arising from a humble heart that turns to God in faith seeking His forgiveness for wrongdoing. For repentance to take place one must have the right heart condition.

From our text in Isaiah 57:15 we find out that though God is High and exalted, He is not far from one who has a repentant heart-broken and contrite heart.

A proud heart will not be able to repent because one with such a heart will not accept responsibility for any wrongdoing. A hardened heart will not accept God's message of salvation (Hebrews 3:15) and an unbelieving heart will not agree with God's Word. We are therefore warned against having such a heart. The appropriate condition for repentance is one that is: humble, broken and contrite, soft-hearted, one with faith in God.

After thoughts: What is the present state of your heart? Be careful that you don't grow hardened or proud in heart as it leads one away from God. True repentance leads us closer to God.

Prayer: Ask God for a new heart one that does not oppose Him and that is not proud but one that can quickly turn to Him in all sincerity and humility.

REPENTANCE; GODLY SORROW

2 Corinthians 7:9-10; Luke 22:60-62

MEMORY VERSE:

> *"Now I am glad, not that you had sorrow, but that*
> *your sorrow was the cause of a change of heart;*
> *for yours was a holy sorrow so that you might*
> *undergo no loss by us in anything."*

> 2 CORINTHIANS 7:9 BBE

We can experience sorrow for various reasons, many people at some point feel bad about their wrongdoing with some sorrowing or grief accompanying it. However, it is not profitable to go sorrowing for our wrongdoing without God in the picture. The absence of God in the midst of sorrow can lead one on to a self-destructive path.

There are two kinds of sorrow, one is worldly and has great potential for harm. Judas Iscariot betrayed the Lord Jesus and got rewarded with some money, afterwards, he felt bad and tried to return the money but was rejected, he threw the money at the scene and went away to his death. He had sorrow for his wrongdoing, but it was not godly. It lacked hope and it involved him trying to save face but not turning to God.

The other kind of sorrow is godly sorrow. This kind of sorrow leads us to change our way of life. It has hope and leads us to God. It was the type of sorrow the Corinthians in our text had after Paul the Apostle wrote to correct them.

After Thoughts: If you feel guilty about any wrongdoing, the right thing to do is turn to God in repentance. You cannot correct your heart by harming yourself. Let your sorrowing, your weeping look up to God in faith and not to yourself in self-condemnation.

Prayer: Lord thank You for teaching true repentance. Save me from every form of self harm. Do not allow me to dwell in sorrow but with hope in Jesus name. Amen.

REPENTANCE; CHANGE IN ATTITUDE AND WAY OF THINKING

Luke 15:11-19

MEMORY VERSE:

> *"I will get up and go to my father, and will say to him, Father, I have done wrong, against heaven and in your eyes:"*

LUKE 15:18 KJV

Repentance involves change in thinking and attitude. The story of the prodigal son paints a picture of a change in thinking and perspective. The word 'repentance' is translated as 'chegáriá' in the Igbo, Nigerian language and it connotes a change in the direction of thinking.

At first the prodigal son treasured the idea of independence from the father. I know some of us have desired the same thing, thinking that we were being restricted and stopped from having real fun. Well in the course of time, the prodigal son squandered all his resources and faced lack and deprivation; he also began having to stay with a certain man who owned pigs and yet got nothing significant from that venture. Eventually, he 'came to his senses' (Luke 15:17) and began to think about all the privileges he had with his father which he had abandoned, most importantly he took responsibility for his actions and was willing, if possible, to pay for it by becoming a servant instead of a son.

Notice that he didn't inflict any punishment on himself but was willing to accept due punishment. His thoughts and attitude had changed, and he decided to go back to his father.

After thoughts: Repentance involves turning away from the thinking that makes us not to own up to our wrong; the thinking and attitude that made us do the wrong in the first place. We instead take responsibility and seek to correct what we have done with those we have wronged. God's laws are for our good, we do ourselves much evil disobeying Him thinking we are being put in bondage by obedience. The prodigal son as we see, did find out that his Father always meant well for him.

Prayer: Father in Heaven, I know now that You mean well for me. I thank You and think differently henceforth. I own up to all my wrongdoing and ask Your forgiveness, please give me a second chance to serve You Lord, in Jesus name. Amen.

DEVO DAY 7:

THE WAY WE LIVE SHOULD SHOW THAT REPENTANCE HAS TAKEN PLACE

Luke 3:3-14; Luke 15:20-24

MEMORY VERSE:

> *"Make clear by your acts that your hearts have been changed;"*

LUKE 3:8 BBE

The prodigal son as we see in Luke 15:20-24 took corresponding steps after the change in his thinking. He got up and went back to his father not to justify himself but to ask his forgiveness. There are fruits of repentance, and these fruits are the new actions and way of life that corresponds to our change.

John the Baptist in Luke 3:3-14 preached the message of repentance and as people showed willingness to change, he challenged them to prove their repentance by showing it practically in their way of life (Luke 3:10-14). Repentance does not end with just good talking and good feeling. Actions should match our words. In the text we see people from different groups asking what they should to do and John telling each group what to do, ranging from kindness to contentment and self-discipline.

After thoughts: What do you think you should do differently? Your fruits will prove your repentance to be genuine.

Prayer: Lord, I pray for Grace to live a life that bears fruits that shows true repentance in Jesus name. Amen.

ACTIVITY:

1. Describe repentance in your own words.
2. What is the right heart condition for repentance?
3. What is worldly sorrow? Give an example of what it can lead to.
4. What does godly sorrow lead to?
5. Our sorrowing should lead us to God. True or False.
6. When Peter denied the Lord in Luke 22:60-62 and wept bitterly, what type of sorrow was his?

WHAT IS SALVATION?

Salvation – the gift that comes through accepting Jesus Christ, the "Ultimate Sacrifice," who brings us back to God, back to who we were created to be, and to Heaven when we die.

WHY do we need Salvation?

God, the Creator of the Universe, walked with Adam and Eve in the Garden.

Adam sinned. Adam's sin separated him and all of his descendants from God.

What is salvation?

Jesus died for your sins.

DEVO DAY 8:

WHEN JESUS GIVES YOU A NEW HEART - THIS IS WHAT HAPPENS:

> *I will give you a new heart and put a new spirit within you. I will take away your heart of stone and give you a heart of flesh. 27 And I will put My Spirit within you and cause you to follow My Laws and be careful to do what I tell you.*
> *Ezekiel 36:26-27 NLV*

 **How would your life change if Jesus gave you a heart of flesh?**

_____

_____

_____

_____

_____

_____

_____

_____

_____

_____

_____

_____

_____

_____

_____

_____

_____

After thoughts: Ask Jesus to forgive you of your sins. Ask Him to be the King of your heart.

WHAT IS WATER BAPTISM?

We now realize that we have sinned. And we know that Jesus is the only answer given to us from God to be free from sin.

We have repented from our sins and asked Jesus into our heart.

Jesus has begun the process of removing our heart of stone and giving us a heart of flesh.

The next step of this process, or as we call it in this book the "Journey to the Rock" is

Water Baptism.

Water baptism is when a believer is immersed in water, symbolizing the death of Jesus and His ressurection.

> *"Repent, and let every one of you be baptized in the name of Jesus Christ for the remission of sins; and you shall receive the gift of the Holy Spirit.*

ACTS 2:38 NKJV

What does the word **remission** mean?

Remission means – to **release from the guilt or penalty** of.

For instance, if you owed a large debt and the person said that you no longer had to pay that debt – then you would have a **remission** of debt.

When Jesus died on the cross for you and I he said that we no longer have to pay the debt of sin.

When we are immersed in water baptism
it is a **symbol of us dying with Jesus on the cross.**

*Or do you not know that as many of us as were
baptized into Christ Jesus were baptized into His
death?*

ROMANS 6:3 NKJV

When we are raised up out of the water
it is a **symbol of Jesus being resurrected.**

*Therefore we were buried with Him through
baptism into death, that just as Christ was
raised from the dead by the glory of the Father,
even so we also should walk in newness of life.*

ROMANS 6:4 NKJV

HOW CAN WE UNDERSTAND "NEW LIFE?"

When we are water baptized, Jesus says to Satan, "**No longer** will you have control over them. When they go down into that water with Me, **everything** that you have in them is gone."

We come up out of that water with new life, we come out a new creature, and we come out **sons of God.**

When we are buried with Jesus by Water Baptism it:

- Destroys the sin nature (the DNA) of Adam.

- Replaces the new nature (the DNA) of Jesus Christ.

For as many of you as were baptized into Christ have put on Christ.

GALATIANS 3:27 NKJV

Therefore, if anyone is in Christ, he is a new creation; old things have passed away; behold, all things have become new.

2 CORINTHIANS 5:17 NKJV

Through water baptism we are no longer slaves to sin, but we are servants of righteousness.

God has given us the answer.

DEVO DAY 9:

WATER BAPTISM; DEATH OF THE OLD LIFE AND A NEW BEGINNING

Romans 6: 3-4

MEMORY VERSE:

> *"And while they were going on their way, they came to some water, and the Ethiopian said, See, here is water; why may I not have baptism?"*

ACTS 8:36 BBE

How do you feel after taking a shower, refreshed and cool, right? This is just one of the things we can do with water in the natural.

However, we have more than that, when we are baptized in water as a proof of our faith in Jesus Christ.

Water baptism is a symbol of what Christ has done for us. When you are immersed in water, it symbolizes your partaking of the death and burial of Christ where the body of sin — the old life, was done away with. When you are raised from the water, it symbolizes your partaking in Jesus Christ's resurrection; that call into a new life. You now are associated with **GOD's own DNA.**

Hallelujah!

The Ethiopian government official (eunuch) after hearing God's message of Salvation and upon seeing a body of water, immediately asked to be baptized because he understood very well what he wanted and its implication.

It was a public declaration of his new found faith and symbolizes what had happened; death of his old life and a resurrection to a new life.

After thoughts: If you have been baptized you now know the reason for it if you didn't know this before now. If you are not yet baptized in water, you can request for it with a clear understanding of what it is all about.

Prayer: Thank You Lord for the water of baptism by which I am baptized into Christ. Help me to continually live in the refreshing life this water brings in Jesus Name. Amen

PHILIP AND THE ETHIOPIAN EUNUCH

1. An angel of the Lord told Philip to go south to the desert road running from Jerusalem to Gaza. Philip obeyed and on the road he saw a chariot. Inside was an important Ethiopian official in charge of the queen's treasury who had gone to Jerusalem to worship and was returning home. The Holy Spirit told Philip, 'Go to that chariot and stay near it.'

2. Philip ran up to the chariot and heard the man reading aloud the words of the prophet Isaiah. (Isaiah 53:7-8).

3. 'Do you understand what you are reading?' Philip asked. 'How can I unless someone explains it to me?' The Ethiopian replied.

4. He invited Philip to sit in the chariot with him.

5. The passage the Ethiopian was reading was about the Saviour God had promised to send. It read, 'He was led like a sheep to the slaughter, and as a lamb before its shearer is silent, so he did not open his mouth.'

6. 'In his humiliation he was deprived of justice.Who can speak of his descendants? For his life was taken from the earth.'

7. 'Please tell me who the prophet is talking about,' the Ethiopian said, 'himself or someone else?'

8. 'The prophet Isaiah is talking about Jesus,' Philip explained. Then he told him how Jesus had died and risen from the dead so anyone could have their sins forgiven.

9. As they travelled along the road the Ethiopian said, 'Look, here is some water. 'What can stop me being baptized?' He gave orders to stop the chariot.'

10. The Ethiopian went into the water where Philip baptized him. As Philip

came out of the water, the Spirit of the Lord took him away and he appeared at Azotus (Ashdod) where he preached in all the towns as he travelled north to Caesarea.

11. The Ethiopian went on his way home rejoicing.

After thoughts: Tell the story on the following pages in your own words. share it with a friend.

Philip and the
Ethiopian Official

Acts 8:26-40

WHO IS THE HOLY SPIRIT?

WHO IS THE HOLY SPIRIT?

Our God is three persons, but one God. The Father, Jesus His Son, and The Holy Spirit.

The Holy Spirit was active in creating the Earth and writing the Bible.

The Holy Spirit loves to teach people about God. He will comfort you when you feel sad.

Holy Spirit loves to help you when you ask him.

WHAT IS THE BAPTISM OF THE HOLY SPIRIT?

After Jesus was killed, he was dead for three days, then His Father made Him come alive again. Then He went back to heaven to be with His Father. Before Jesus went to heaven, he spent 40 days with his students. He promised to send the Holy Spirit to be with them so they would not be alone.

After Jesus left, The Holy Spirit came to Jesus' students who were together praying, and He baptized them with power and boldness. It was such an amazing experience. They began boldly preaching about Jesus in languages they had never learned and made sick people well.

Now they would not be afraid or alone because the Holy Spirit came to live inside of them, so He was always with them.

Jesus' promise is for you too! You can have the baptism of the Holy Spirit too if you ask Him.

ANOTHER BAPTISM AFTER WATER BAPTISM

Matthew 3:11; Acts 19:1-6

MEMORY VERSE:

> "*I indeed baptize you with water unto repentance,
> but He who is coming after me is mightier than
> I, whose sandals I am not worthy to carry. He
> will baptize you with the Holy Spirit and fire.*"

MATTHEW 3:11 NKJV

Acts 19:1-6 narrates the experience of a group of young converts to Christianity who knew water baptism; the one done by John the Baptist. Water baptism as we had discussed earlier symbolizes the new life in Christ however, we are promised another baptism to be carried out by Christ Himself. It is the baptism of the Holy Spirit.

All who receive God's call to salvation are to desire the baptism of the Holy Spirit. It is so important, and it is not for a select few.

Unlike water baptism you do not need to go to a particular location to be baptized with the Holy Spirit. You can always receive Him when you ask in faith as a Pastor prays for you, or as you hear the Word preached, in a public meeting or during your private prayer time.

After thoughts: The early church ensured that new believers got baptized with water as well as with the Holy Spirit.

Prayer: Thank You Lord for the baptism of the Holy Spirit.

BAPTISM OF THE HOLY SPIRIT; RECEIVING POWER

Acts 1:8; Acts 2:1-12

MEMORY VERSE:

> *"But you will have power, when the Holy Spirit has come on you; and you will be my witnesses in Jerusalem and all Judaea and Samaria, and to the ends of the earth."*

> ACTS. 1:8 BBE

Without power, any work will be frustrating and burdensome. Attempting to do God's work without the Holy Spirit is attempting to do God's work without His Power. We receive power when the Holy Spirit comes upon us. That is the whole essence of the baptism of the Holy Spirit. With Him we have the identity that we belong to God (Romans 8:9) and can be His witnesses (represent Him, presenting His gospel to others)

When the Holy Spirit came upon the earliest disciples: they spoke with other tongues (languages) telling of the wondrous works of God and had tongues of fire appear visibly on their head, we are not to expect to see physical fire fall on us before we believe that we have received the His baptism. We should know that with the Holy Spirit baptism we will praise God more abundantly exclaiming his praise in unknown languages or tongues and having the boldness to preach as well as living a victorious and glorious life as long as we continue to trust Him. (Acts 4:31).

With this empowerment by the Holy Spirit, we can go on to do Christian service and reach out to our world.

After thoughts: Do you think that you can really do God's work without His Power? Jesus emphasized the Holy Spirit Baptism and so should we.

Prayer: Lord, please baptize me with Your Spirit as promised in Your word in Jesus name. Amen

BAPTISM OF THE HOLY SPIRIT; THINGS YOU SHOULD KNOW

Luke 11:13; Acts 2:38-39

MEMORY VERSE:

> *"You are sinful and you know how to give good things to your children. How much more will your Father in heaven give the Holy Spirit to those who ask Him?"*

LUKE 11:13 NLV

There are misconceptions about the baptism of the Holy Spirit, but God's word does not leave us in doubt about what we should do and expect. Here are few things we should know as revealed in God's word:

1. God is a good God and does not give evil gifts. The gift of the Holy Spirit is God's gift to the believer and in Him is no evil. (James 1:17; Luke 11:13)

2. God is very willing to give us the Holy Spirit; we are only to ask and believe. Our earthly parents would often give us what we ask how much more our heavenly Father. (Luke 11:9-13)

3. The Baptism is for all believers and not for a select few. (Acts 2:39)

4. One primary evidence of the baptism of the Holy Spirit, is that we speak with new tongues and magnify God. So, you don't go about seeking tongues, but seek the Holy Spirit and He will give you utterance to speak. You don't need to copy anyone but trust Him to give you utterance. (Acts 2:1-4; Acts 10:44-46)

5. The Baptism of the Holy Spirit must not always be so dramatic. God can choose to baptize anyone in any meeting with or without so much spectacular manifestations. However, a common experience is speaking in tongues, boldness, and power to do Christian service as we see in the experience of the apostles. (Acts 4:8-13)

Prayer: Lord rid me of any misconceptions about the Holy Spirit that has hindered my accepting Him in Jesus name Amen.

BAPTISM OF THE HOLY SPIRIT; HOW TO RECEIVE HIM

Acts 2:1-4; Acts 10:44-46; Acts 19:6

MEMORY VERSE:

> *"Then Peter said unto them, Repent, and be baptized every one of you in the name of Jesus Christ for the remission of sins, and ye shall receive the gift of the Holy Ghost."*

ACTS 2:39 KJV

The primary qualification for receiving the Holy Spirit is that you are saved. God is not restricted by methods the common factor is the presence of faith whether in the assembly of believers or in a private place, the baptism of the Holy Spirit can take place once faith is present.

Possible situations during which one can receive the Holy Spirit

- Through laying on of hands by an anointed Minister. (Acts 9:17; Acts 19:6)
- During a period of waiting on the Lord. (Acts 2:1-4)
- During a Christian Meeting where the word of God is being preached. (Acts 10:44-46)
- During or after private or public prayer. (Acts 4:31)
- The experience of people who received the Holy Spirit Baptism varies from person to person; Cornelius and his family received the baptism of the Holy Spirit while Peter yet preached the word of God to them. Paul the Apostle had a disciple named Ananias lay hands on him, while the first group of believers (this included Jesus' disciples) who received the baptism of the Holy Spirit were waiting on the Lord as He had instructed them when the baptism of the Holy Spirit took place.

After thoughts: You too can receive Him. You don't have to travel far, if you have faith and ask the Father, He will give it to you.

Prayer: Help me Lord to know how to use my faith in receiving the Holy Spirit in Jesus name Amen.

DEVO DAY 10:

MOVING FORWARD AFTER THE BAPTISM OF THE HOLY SPIRIT

Galatians 3:2-5

MEMORY VERSE:

> *"But you, beloved, building yourselves up on your most holy faith, praying in the Holy Spirit,"*

JUDE 20 NKJV

Now that you have received the baptism of the Holy Spirit, what next? You are to continue in the Spirit; the life of the Spirit is a life of faith. One way to build up your faith is by praying in the Holy Ghost as our memory verse admonishes. Praying in the Holy Ghost simply means praying by the leading of the Spirit and this can be in an unknown tongue or with understanding (language you can understand) the central truth nevertheless is that such prayers are not from the mind or intellect. They may not even make sense at the moment so to say but they are always the appropriate prayers at the time, and these will constitute a major part of the prayers you will need as you continue the spiritual walk.

Don't get discouraged as you may not understand everything yet, however, make sure you continue to study the word and pray. The Holy Spirit, Who is now in you, will help teach you. Also never neglect Christian fellowship meetings and or Church services; these are avenues through which God will help you and cause you to grow. As you do these you will soon begin to discover your spiritual gifts, these will be more evident as you serve your local church or Christian fellowship.

After thoughts: If you started in the Spirit would you make it if you decide to live by the flesh? Certainly not! Continue the walk in the Spirit it is a walk in faith and soon you will become more and more fruitful in God's House.

Prayer: Righteous Father, as I have been ushered into a life in the Spirit help me not to go back or seek to end my journey in the flesh in Jesus name Amen.

WHAT MUST I DO TO BE SAVED?

Pray this prayer:

Dear Jesus, I know that I have sinned; I have chosen to do things that are wrong when I could have chosen the right way. I repent from those sins; I want and need my life to change... Today. Please forgive me and place your new heart and your new spirit within me. Please come and live in my heart forever. Jesus, please fill my heart with your love and compassion for others and guide me all of the days of my life. Amen.

Now, look for a church that believes in the Bible as the Word of God. Find out what the next steps are to be a Christian, follow Jesus, know God as your King, and be led by His Spirit.

HOW can we protect such a great gift?

Spend good time with God and other Believers

Walk in the Light

Keep confessing your sins

Spend time reading your Bible

Pray daily

DEVO DAY: 11

WHAT MUST I DO TO BE SAVED?

Acts 16:16-34; Romans 10:9-10

MEMORY VERSE:

"So they said, "Believe on the Lord Jesus Christ, and you will be saved, you and your household."

ACTS 16:31 NKJV

'What must I do to be saved' is a serious question and it will be topmost in the heart of anyone in serious trouble. However, some problems and situations are beyond man's ability and except God intervenes in such situations, one may be doomed.

In the ancient times, prison guards under whose watch there was a prison break risked death (Acts 12:19). So, we see the jailer in our text upon realising that the jail doors were open attempt to kill himself but was stopped by the Apostle Paul who assured him that none of the prisoners had escaped. Trembling, he regretted his earlier actions and came face to face with the reality of Salvation asking to know what he must do to be saved. He must have wondered what was the Hope of Paul and Silas that made them sing when in prison. Certainly, it was something worth having.

Are you like the jailer today? Do you think you have no hope whatsoever? Wait a minute! There is hope, believe in the Lord Jesus Christ and you will be saved. Call upon Jesus now. The jailer believed and was saved ultimately from eternal doom.

After thoughts: You too can believe today and see Jesus turn around your life for good. When we believe in Christ Jesus; we agree with all He has done already for us and partake in His victorious living. Talk to the Lord in Faith

Prayer: Lord, I believe in You. I believe in Jesus. I am saved in Jesus name. I am free in Jesus name. Amen.

GO MAKE DISCIPLES

A disciple is a follower or student of a teacher.

When Jesus called his disciples, he simply said,

> *"Follow me and **I will make you** fishers of men"*
>
> MATTHEW 4:19 KJV

Jesus taught them to do everything He did, to heal every kind of sickness, cast out devils, and preach about the Kingdom of Heaven.

Just before Jesus went to heaven, He told His disciples to tell the whole world the good news.

BUT, How can you follow a God you cannot see?

Follow the Bible. This is our instruction book to teach us what is right. It is God's letter to us.

Follow the Holy Spirit who gives us personal direction since He lives inside of us now.

It is natural for you to hear God's voice and be led by the Holy Spirit.

God loves people so much that Jesus died for them. He wants you to tell people and make disciples of those who will believe your words.

MEMORY VERSE:

"Go, preach, teach, and baptize and make disciples of all nations."

MATTHEW 28:19, MARK 16:15-16

DEVO DAY 12:

GO MAKE DISCIPLES

Mathew 28:18-20

MEMORY VERSE:

*"Go ye therefore, and teach all nations, baptizing
them in the name of the Father, and of the Son,
and of the Holy Ghost: teaching them to observe
all things whatsoever I have commanded you:
and, lo, I am with you alway, even unto the end
of the world. Amen."*

MATHEW 28:18-19 KJV

Have you ever been to a place where you enjoyed every bit of your stay and wished some of your friends would have the same treat? When you got back home to your friends, you realised you could not resist the urge to tell them about your experience. God's message of salvation is more than just a nice treat. It is the best news of all time; that if you have Christ, you have Hope eternal life. So, we are not just obliged as believers, to share God's message but commanded by Jesus Himself to do so.

When we share the gospel with others, we are working to make disciples who will become new members of God's family. They in turn together with us will affect our world positively to the glory of God. Disciples are people who follows certain teaching and tenets. God is calling you and I not just to be His disciples but add to the number by bringing more to the family.

After thoughts: If you have unbelievers or rebellious people in your family you can believe God for their salvation because He is not just interested in the salvation of individuals alone but whole families.

Action Points: Share the good news as often as possible; talk to that relative, that friend, that neighbour.

Prayer: Lord thank You for the opportunity to participate in making disciples. Help me to be courageous and to be obedient to your command. Let men from every nation and tribe come to You in Jesus name. Amen.

ACTIVITY:

This can be done as a project for a whole year

- Write down names of those you talk to daily.
- Look at it weekly pray for them.

DAILY PLAN

DATE: / /

NOTE

MONTHLY PLAN

MONTH:

1 2 3 4 5 6 7 8 9 10 11 12 13 14 15 16 17 18 19 20 21 22 23 24 25 26 27 28 29 30 31

_____ ○○○○○○○○○○○○○○○○○○○○○○○○○○○○○○○
_____ ○○○○○○○○○○○○○○○○○○○○○○○○○○○○○○○
_____ ○○○○○○○○○○○○○○○○○○○○○○○○○○○○○○○
_____ ○○○○○○○○○○○○○○○○○○○○○○○○○○○○○○○

NOTE

FILL IN THE BLANKS

ACROSS

3. We are Created in God's _____

9. Name of garden Adam and Eve were placed in

10. Created on first day

11. How to receive the Holy Spirit

12. God's enemy's name

13. God is all _____

15. What God did on 7th day

16. Go and _____ all nations

17. What a follower is called

19. Another name for Satan

21. Where God lives

DOWN

1. Belief and trust in God

2. God wants to _____ with us

4. God's enemy is _____

5. We need a new _____

6. Sin nature from Adam

7. The man God created

8. Talking with God

13. Made by God

14. Where God walked with Adam

18. Separates us from God

20. The woman God formed

FREELY YOU HAVE RECEIVED, FREELY GIVE

MEMORY VERSE:

Go ye therefore, and teach all nations, baptizing them in the name of the Father, and of the Son, and of the Holy Ghost: 20 Teaching them to observe all things whatsoever I have commanded you: and, lo, I am with you always, [even] unto the end of the world.

MATTHEW 28:19

ANSWERS

Puzzle: Which Day did God Create:

1. Light
2. The Heavens
3. Earth, Sea, Vegetation
4. Sun Moon and Stars
5. Birds and Sea Animals
6. Land Animals and Adam
7. Rest

Puzzle: In the Beginning

S	D	R	I	B	K	K	B	O	W	G	N	A	M
O	S	T	S	S	E	N	K	R	A	D	T	T	E
B	M	E	S	E	O	O	D	N	D	D	I	H	N
D	S	Y	A	D	N	E	V	E	S	U	L	E	E
G	E	I	G	H	E	A	V	E	N	S	A	W	G
E	P	K	N	N	P	N	G	N	T	D	O	O	H
A	A	H	I	T	R	A	E	H	E	R	D	R	V
I	R	S	N	B	A	D	N	L	R	A	M	D	U
N	A	D	N	E	L	A	I	E	D	O	R	E	O
D	T	A	I	B	O	T	N	S	D	N	H	R	N
B	E	S	G	I	V	S	O	G	T	K	E	N	O
T	D	S	E	B	E	G	N	M	P	E	L	O	D
I	S	G	B	L	L	I	E	O	E	R	A	T	N
O	N	D	N	E	K	T	A	A	N	S	W	R	R

Puzzle: Nations of the World

```
N K S E N I P P I L I H P R
I R U S S I A D A N A C A I
N A T I V E A M E R I C A N
A M C L B B R A Z I L E H S
P N H E E A D N A L I A H T
G E I A L U R E P Y N N G M
A D L R E P I B A B D E E E
E R E S E O E D A I I D R X
E T H I O P I A Y D A E M I
C N K E N Y A I D J O W A C
N N A M I B I A S N A S N O
A Z A E J O R D A N A P Y R
R A A R G E N T I N A G A U
F S E T A T S D E T I N U N
```

Puzzle: Is it Sin?

```
G S T F A R C H C T I W S D
F A L S E T E A C H I N G S
I G N I Y L M U R D E R S S
Y J I D O L A T R Y A R S S
G O O D N E S S F A I T H E
E N V Y F C L O V E N I H L
I S G U R D F O E S U B A F
E L N O I T A C I N R O F I
S Y S H A T R E D A E N L S
W I L D P A R T I E S E W H
N H G N I T H G I F N R S N
M E E K N E S S T T S U L E
A N G R Y O U T B U R S T S
E K E D R U N K E N N E S S
```

Foundations of Faith Crossword Puzzle

Across

3. image

9. Eden

10. Light

11. Ask

12. Satan

13. Colors

15. Rested

16. Teach

17. Disciples

19. Evil

21. Heaven

Down

1. Faith

2. live

4. evil

5. Heart

6. DNA

7. Adam

8. Prayer

13. Eve

ACKNOWLEDGEMENTS

Images used with permission from book "God Saw That It Was Good" by Danny Bravin and Teresa Skinner. Pages 3, 4 and 17.

Free Bibleimages have been granted permission to make these images freely available for personal, teaching and ministry use under a Creative Commons Attribution-NonCommercial-NoDerivatives 4.0 International License.

Image made possible by a joint venture of Good News Productions, International and College Press Publishing Co. Artist: Paula Nash Giltner www.theglobalgospel.org

Philip and the Ethiopian Eunuch

Original illustrations are the copyright of Sweet Publishing and these digitally adjusted compilations of them the copyright of FreeBibleimages. They are made available for free download under a Creative Commons Attribution-ShareAlike 3.0 Unported license.

www.ingramcontent.com/pod-product-compliance
Lightning Source LLC
Chambersburg PA
CBHW071105120626
46546CB00003B/1275